HOME COOKING WITH EN

HOME COOKING WITH ENA

ENA THOMAS

Photography by:
Mair, Over the Moon Photography & Design,
Swansea

HUGHES

First printed: February 1999

ISBN 0 85284 241 4

Co-ordinated by: Luned Whelan.

Typeset and printed in Wales by
Dinefwr Press, Rawlings Road,
Llandybïe, Carmarthenshire, SA18 3YD.

Published by Hughes a'i Fab
S4C International, 50 Lambourne Crescent,
Cardiff Business Park,
Llanishen, Cardiff, CF4 5WJ.

CONTENTS

ACKNOWLEDGEMENTS

Thanks are due to the following people who helped in the making of this book: Geoff Thomas, for his support and his computer skills; Mair and Siân for the photos; Eleri Huws for her eagle editorial eye; the team at Dinefwr Press, and Luned Whelan, for overseeing the project and being so willing to taste the food!

FOREWORD

I have been interested in cooking for the whole of my adult life, and I have seen many changes over the years. The recent developments in the food industry in Wales have been astounding, and the idea for this book arose from the sheer variety and quality of the Welsh ingredients that are now available, many of which I have used on **Heno**.

Wales has long been associated with leeks, *bara brith* and beer, but that has changed dramatically with the advent of Welsh cheeses, wines, meat, fish and seafood gaining an international reputation for the highest quality products.

The Llangollen Food Festival, started in 1998, was the perfect platform to show the diversity of the development of the industry. From organic ostriches to cheeses being supplied to supermarket chains; from honey products to home-made mustards, the breadth of choice was obvious and deserved much praise.

The recipes in this book are mainly based around Welsh ingredients. Where none is specified, it is your challenge to find a Welsh version of any given product! Some of the recipes are from other countries as far afield as Morocco and Spain, and this shows how confident we can be of our products here in Wales, by not being afraid to welcome outside influences.

I hope that wherever you are using this book, you can reflect Wales in your kitchen and enjoy its flavours for a long time to come.

Iechyd da!

ENA

CONVERSION TABLES

The following are all approximate measurements, which have been either rounded up or down. You should make it a practice that you never mix imperial and metric measurements in any recipe; always adhere to one standard.

MEASUREMENTS

⅛ inch	3mm
¼ inch	5mm
½ inch	1.2cm
1 inch	2.5cm
1¼ inch	3cm
1½ inch	4cm
1¾ inch	4.5cm
2 inch	5cm
2½ inch	6cm
3 inch	7.5cm
3½ inch	9cm
4 inch	10cm
5 inch	13cm
5½ inch	13.5cm
6 inch	15cm
6½ inch	16cm
7 inch	18cm
7½ inch	19cm
8 inch	20cm
9 inch	23cm
9½ inch	24cm
10 inch	25.5cm
11 inch	28cm
12 inch	30cm

VOLUME

2 flu oz	55ml
3 flu oz	75ml
5 flu oz (¼ pint)	150ml
½ pint	275ml
¾ pint	425ml
1 pint	570ml
1½ pints	725ml
1¾ pints	1 litre
2 pints	1.1 litre
2½ pints	1.4 litre
4 pints	2.25 litre

WEIGHTS

½ oz	10g
¾ oz	15g
1 oz	25g
1½ oz	40g
2 oz	50g
2½ oz	65g
3 oz	75g
4 oz	110g
4½ oz	125g
5 oz	150g
6 oz	175g
7 oz	200g
8 oz	225g
9 oz	250g
10 oz	275g
12 oz	350g
1 lb	450g
1½ lb	700g
2 lb	900g
3 lb	1.35kg

OVEN TEMPERATURES

140C	275F	Mark 1
150C	300F	Mark 2
170C	325F	Mark 3
180C	350F	Mark 4
190C	375F	Mark 5
200C	400F	Mark 6
220C	425F	Mark 7
230C	450F	Mark 8
240C	475F	Mark 9

STARTERS

There is something for everyone in this chapter – meat-eaters, vegetarians, fans of fish and soups. It is wholly appropriate that my recipe for Cawl is the first of many recipes using Welsh ingredients throughout the book. Enjoy!

ENA'S *CAWL*

Cawl *is perhaps the most Welsh of dishes, and there are as many varieties as there are cooks! It is a little healthier now than it was in the old days, when fat would be floating on top! This can be made as a vegetarian recipe as well, omitting the meat and adding some pre-soaked pulses.*

Ingredients
900g/2 lb shin of beef
450g/1 lb potatoes, cut into chunks
350g/12oz carrots, cut into chunks
350g/12oz parsnips, cut into chunks
350g/12oz swedes, cut into chunks
2 onions, chopped
salt and pepper
450g/1 lb leeks, thoroughly washed and cut in chunks
good bunch of parsley, chopped

Method
- Place the meat in a large saucepan with the onions. Cover with water, bring to the boil, cover and simmer for about 2 hours.
- Leave overnight to cool completely, then remove any excess fat from the top. Remove the meat from the stock onto a plate.
- Add the prepared vegetables to the stock, bring to the boil and simmer for about 30 minutes.
- Add the leeks and cook for a further 5 minutes.
- Add the chopped parsley and seasoning. Cut the meat into chunks, add to the vegetables and stock and heat through before serving.

AVOCADO PÂTÉ

This recipe is very quick and easy to make, livening up the taste of avocado, which can be quite bland. I must say I find this pâté just heavenly! Ideal for a quick snack or as a starter.

Ingredients
2 medium avocados
2 cloves garlic
225g/8 oz Welsh cream cheese
2-3 drops Tabasco sauce
juice of 1 lemon
ground black pepper

Method
- Cut the avocados in half lengthways and remove the stone, then scoop out the flesh.

- Place the avocado, garlic, cream cheese, Tabasco sauce, lemon juice and a little black pepper into a food processor and process for 1-2 minutes until smooth.

- To serve: either fill the empty avocado shells with the pâté, or fill little ramekin dishes. Garnish with lemon and serve with crusty bread or Melba toast.

- Note: the mixture is easier to process if the cheese has been slightly softened beforehand.

STUFFED TOMATOES

Tomatoes are available all year round now, and are very versatile, but in my opinion you cannot beat the flavour when they are in season. This is a great dish for both meat-eaters and vegetarians.

Ingredients
4 large beef tomatoes
1 stick celery
1 small red apple
110g/4 oz cooked chicken, ham or cheese
small bunch fresh chives
a little chopped parsley
1 clove garlic, crushed
110g/4 oz mayonnaise
salt and pepper

Method
- Cut a slice off the tomato where the stalk is.
- Remove all the seeds, then place the tomatoes upside down on a plate to drain.
- Chop the celery finely, core the apple and chop finely.
- Cut the chicken, ham or cheese into small pieces.
- Mix all the ingredients together and season to taste. Spoon the filling into the tomato shells and replace the tops.
- Serve with a light crispy green salad.

CRAB AND SALMON MOUSSE

A delicious and easy starter.

Ingredients
225g/8 oz fresh or tinned crab
225g/8 oz fresh or tinned salmon
4 tablespoons seafood dressing
350g/12 oz cream cheese
juice and rind of 1 lemon

Method
- Drain the crab and salmon well if using tinned fish.

- Place the fish in a food processor with the cream cheese, lemon juice and rind, and the seafood dressing.

- Process for 1 minute. If your food processor is small, divide the mixture in two and whizz both lots, then mix together.

- Serve in ramekin dishes with shredded lettuce, cucumber and tomato.

LUXURY WELSH RAREBIT

Welsh rarebit is one of my favourite snacks, and very easy to make. If you're keeping an eye on your waistline, use low-fat versions of the cream and cheese!

Ingredients
150ml/¼ pint double cream
175g/6 oz mature Welsh cheddar cheese, grated
½ teaspoon paprika
1 teaspoon mustard
4 rounds of toast
salt and pepper

Method
- Place the cream and grated cheese into a heavy-based saucepan and gently bring to the boil. It should be of a thick consistency.

- Add the paprika, mustard, salt and pepper into the mixture.

- Spread the rarebit thickly on the four rounds of toast and pop under the grill to brown.

- Serve with a garnish of grilled tomatoes and sprinkle with parsley.

- Note: this recipe is even better if it is prepared the previous day and left to thicken. Cover, and keep in the fridge for up to three days.

HOT POTATO, BACON AND TOMATO SALAD

This is a delightful way of serving new potatoes and baby tomatoes.

Ingredients
450g/1 lb small new potatoes
450g/1 lb baby tomatoes
1 tablespoon chopped parsley and mint
110g/4 oz smoked bacon
salt and pepper

Method
- Scrub the potatoes until clean, place into cold water, bring to the boil and cook for 15 minutes. Drain and keep warm.

- Remove the skins of the tomatoes by plunging them into boiling water for 2-3 seconds, making them easy to skin.

- Chop the bacon into small pieces and fry in a little oil until crisp.

- To the potatoes, add the bacon, tomatoes, parsley and mint, and season to taste.

- Sprinkle with freshly ground black pepper to serve.

WELSH CHEESE AND HERB PÂTÉ

This recipe makes a quick and tasty snack, and is ideal for serving on toast, to make canapés or as a jacket potato topping.

Ingredients
450g/1 lb good Welsh cream cheese
juice of 1 lemon
pinch of grated nutmeg
1 tablespoon creamed horseradish sauce
50g/2 oz melted butter
2-3 cloves garlic, crushed
1 tablespoon chopped fresh parsley and chives

Method
- Place the cheese, lemon juice, nutmeg, horseradish sauce, garlic and the cooled melted butter in a large bowl.

- Mix well, making sure the ingredients are evenly distributed.

- Line a 700g/1½ lb loaf tin with clingfilm, spoon in the cheese mixture and even out the top with a palette knife.

- Cover with clingfilm and leave to set overnight in the fridge.

SPICY FISH CAKES

A quick, easy recipe, perfect for busy mothers running a home and a job, with limited time to spend in the kitchen.

Ingredients
400g/14 oz tin of tuna or salmon
110g/4 oz sesame seeds
1 teaspoon minced ginger
1 teaspoon chilli powder
3 spring onions, finely sliced
450g/1 lb mashed potatoes
3-4 tablespoons mayonnaise
1 tablespoon chopped parsley
olive oil for frying
salt and pepper

Method
- Place the mashed potatoes in a large bowl.
- Add the ginger, chilli powder, flaked tuna, spring onions, parsley and mayonnaise. Season to taste.
- Mix well until all the ingredients are blended. Take a small handful of the mixture at a time and shape into cakes.
- Toss the cakes in the sesame seeds, heat the oil in a large frying-pan and cook the fish cakes for 2-3 minutes each side.
- Serve with salad or chips.
- Note: instant mashed potato can be used.

PUMPKIN SOUP

Excellent for Hallowe'en, this is made with the traditional bright orange pumpkin. As pumpkin is quite bland, you need to add a fair amount of herbs and spices to bring out the flavour.

Ingredients
700g-900g/1½-2 lb pumpkin flesh, chopped
1 tablespoon olive oil
50g/2 oz butter
1 onion, chopped
2 carrots, chopped
2 potatoes, chopped
2 sticks celery, chopped
425ml/¾ pint vegetable or chicken stock
1 teaspoon minced ginger
1 teaspoon grated nutmeg
1 teaspoon ground coriander
1 tablespoon tomato purée
450g/1 lb cooking apples, chopped
1 lemon
salt and pepper

Method
- Heat the oil and butter in a large saucepan, and add the pumpkin flesh, the chopped vegetables and apples, and the spices.

- Cook them covered over a low heat until the pumpkin flesh and apples are very soft.

- Pour in the stock and tomato purée, bring to the boil and simmer for 15 minutes.

- Liquidise the soup, check for seasoning and mix in the juice of the lemon. Reheat and serve with a little sour cream and crusty bread. Garnish with parsley.

- Note: for a party, use the empty pumpkin shell as your serving bowl!

CELERIAC AND APPLE SOUP

This soup is delicious – I love the texture of the celeriac. It can be served hot or cold, and it is suitable for lunch or supper as well as a starter.

Ingredients
450g/1 lb celeriac
450g/1 lb cooking apples
225g/8 oz onions
110g/4 oz butter
1 tablespoon chopped chives and parsley
725ml/1½ pints chicken or vegetable stock
salt and pepper

Method
- Peel the onions, celeriac and apples, then cut into small pieces.

- Melt the butter in a large saucepan and gently fry the onions for 2-3 minutes.

- Add the celeriac and the apples, pour in the stock and bring to the boil.

- Cover and simmer for about 30 minutes until the vegetables are cooked.

- Liquidise the soup until it is all well blended. Taste for seasoning.

- To serve: garnish with chives and parsley, and add a little yogurt or cream if desired.

SUPPERS

Even the most enthusiastic of cooks will sometimes get stuck in a routine, preparing the same kind of meal most evenings. It's not easy, in today's busy times, to shop and prepare and then cook, especially if you're working. I hope that this chapter will give you a few new ideas, or perhaps even inspire you to use these recipes as a base from which to be inventive yourselves!

GLAZED WELSH SHORT BACK BACON

I would normally only think of baking and glazing ham, not bacon. However, a while ago, I bought a piece of Welsh short back bacon, and thought it would be lovely baked with honey or Demerara sugar. Here's the result – I hope you enjoy it as much as I did!

Ingredients
1.35kg/3 lb piece of Welsh short back bacon
2 tablespoons honey or Demerara sugar
4-5 cloves
1 bayleaf
sprig of fresh thyme
275ml/½ pint apple juice or water
275ml/½ pint double cream

Method
- If the bacon is salted, soak it overnight.

- Remove the skin of the bacon joint, then score the fat with a sharp knife.

- Place the bacon in a roasting pan, then pour the honey over it, or rub in the Demerara sugar.

- Pour in the apple juice or water, and add the cloves, bayleaf and thyme.

- Cover with foil and place in the oven at 200C/400F/Gas 6. Bake for about 45 minutes, then remove the foil and bake for a further 30 minutes until the bacon joint looks beautifully glazed.

- To make a sauce from the juices: skim most of the fat away and drain the juices into a saucepan. Pour in the double cream. Bring to the boil, and it is ready to serve with the hot joint.

- This dish is also delicious served cold, thinly sliced with salad and boiled parsley potatoes.

STIR-FRY CHICKEN IN A TOMATO AND ROSEMARY SAUCE

Ingredients
4 chicken breasts
2 packets ready-made tomato and rosemary sauce
1 bunch spring onions
175g/6 oz button mushrooms
2 tablespoons brandy
2 tablespoons oil

Method
- Cut the chicken into strips. Heat a little oil in a pan and quickly stir-fry the chicken for 3-4 minutes.

- Slice the spring onions and mushrooms, and add to the chicken. Cook for a further 3-4 minutes.

- Pour in the sauce and brandy. Bring to the boil and simmer for 5 minutes. Season to taste.

- Garnish with chopped parsley and serve with rice or noodles.

WELSH LAMB IN PEPPER, CHILLI AND GARLIC SAUCE

This is a delightful way of cooking lamb and, as a bonus, it only takes 20 minutes to cook!

Ingredients
1 small leg of lamb
2 packets ready-made tomato, pepper, chilli and garlic sauce
1 tablespoon oil
175g/6 oz long grain rice

Method
- Remove the meat off the bone. Cut the lamb into 5cm/2" pieces, removing all the outer skin.

- Heat the oil in a large pan, and quickly fry the lamb until brown all over.

- Add the rice and the sauce, mix thoroughly and bring to the boil.

- Simmer for 10-15 minutes until the lamb and the rice are cooked.

- Taste for seasoning and garnish with parsley.

PINEAPPLE SPICY PORK TENDERLOIN

Pork is surprisingly low in fat, versatile and simply delicious!

Ingredients
700g/1½ lb pork tenderloin
425g/15 oz tin pineapple pieces in natural juice
½ teaspoon cumin
½ teaspoon coriander
½ teaspoon turmeric
½ teaspoon garam masala
2 tablespoon olive oil
2 cloves garlic, crushed
2 tablespoons mango chutney
1 red pepper cut in half, seeds removed and thinly sliced
225g/8 oz button mushrooms
1 tablespoon Demerara sugar
parsley to garnish

Method
- Slice the pork tenderloin into 5cm/2" pieces.

- Heat the oil in a large frying pan and quickly fry the pork on a high heat until brown all over.

- Add the garlic and spices to the pan, lowering the heat. Cook for 2-3 minutes, stirring occasionally.

- Stir in the pineapple and juice, chutney, mushrooms, sugar and pepper. Stir well, bring to the boil and simmer for 15-20 minutes until the pork is cooked and the sauce is thick and glossy.

- Garnish with the parsley and serve with rice, pasta or green vegetables.

PEPPER SOUP WITH ORGANIC YOGURT AND SODA BREAD

Soup and home-made bread have been a part of Welsh food culture for centuries. Even today, very few suppers are quite so satisfying. Soda bread is perfect for people with a yeast allergy, which is quite common.

Ingredients
3 large red peppers
3 sticks celery, chopped
1 large onion, chopped
2 cloves garlic, crushed
rind of 1 lemon
1 tablespoon chopped thyme
1 tablespoon chopped basil
3 tablespoons olive oil
570ml/1 pint tomato passata
725ml/1½ pints vegetable stock
salt and pepper

Soda Bread
225g/8 oz plain flour
450g/1 lb wholemeal flour
1 teaspoon sea salt
1 teaspoon cream of tartar
1 teaspoon bicarbonate of soda
570ml/1 pint sour milk or buttermilk

The Yogurt Dressing
150ml/¼ pint carton of natural
   organic yogurt
a little lemon juice

pinch cayenne pepper
1 teaspoon chopped basil
  and parsley

Method

- To make the soup: cut the peppers in half and remove the core and seeds. Brush the skin with olive oil and grill for 3-4 minutes. Remove the skin and chop the peppers.

- Heat the remaining oil in a large pan and fry the onions, garlic and celery for 3-4 minutes, then add the peppers.

- Add the thyme, basil, passata, stock and seasoning. Stir well, bring to the boil and simmer for 20 minutes.

- Transfer the soup to a blender and whizz for 2-3 minutes, taking care that you do not overfill the container. Blend in two lots if necessary.

- Adjust the seasoning and serve with the yogurt and soda bread.

- To make the yogurt dressing: mix all the ingredients well, and leave to marinade for a few hours before using.

- To make the soda bread: place all the dry ingredients in a large bowl and mix well using only your fingertips.

- Make a well in the centre and add the milk, mixing until the dough leaves the bowl clean. Knead lightly into a round shape, then flatten slightly and cut a cross in the top.

- Place on a greased baking tray and brush with milk or a beaten egg.

- Cook for 30 minutes at 200C/400F/Gas 6. After 30 minutes, turn upside down and cook for a further 5 minutes.

- When cooked, the loaf should sound hollow when tapped.

- Serve hot or cold with the soup, or for breakfast as a treat.

CHICKEN AND RICE TAGINE

This is a Moroccan recipe which I demonstrated on Heno *when looking at African cuisine. A tagine is a heavy cooking pot, used to keep all the flavour in without letting steam evaporate into the atmosphere. A heatproof casserole dish will perform the same function, so it makes an ideal substitute for a tagine.*

Ingredients
4 chicken breasts, skin removed
1 large onion, finely chopped
2 cloves garlic, crushed
175g/6 oz streaky bacon, chopped
110g/4 oz long grain wild rice
400g/14 oz tin chopped tomatoes
1 teaspoon ground paprika
1 teaspoon ground turmeric
1 teaspoon minced ginger
275ml/½ pint chicken stock
50g/2 oz flaked almonds
1 teaspoon salt
1 tablespoon olive oil
1 tablespoon parsley, finely chopped

Method
- Heat the oil in a tagine or heatproof casserole dish.

- Cut the chicken into bite-size pieces and fry for 2-3 minutes.

- Add the onion, bacon, garlic and spices and cook for a further 3-4 minutes.

- Add the tomatoes, stock, rice and salt. Stir well and gently bring to the boil. Cover and leave to cook for 30-40 minutes.

- Garnish with the parsley and almonds and serve hot.

SMOKED SALMON SURPRISE PARCELS

Ingredients
225g/8 oz thinly sliced smoked salmon
4 eggs
1 shredded lettuce
1 sliced cucumber
4 pineapple rings
a bunch of chives, finely chopped
ground black pepper

Method
- Poach the eggs in simmering hot water for about 5 minutes until the yolk is hard. Remove from the water and place on kitchen paper to absorb any excess moisture.

- Arrange the salmon into four squares, with the slices slightly overlapping.

- Sprinkle with ground black pepper then place the egg on the salmon and fold the salmon around the egg to form a parcel.

- Serve on a pineapple ring, garnished with lettuce, cucumber and chives.

BAKED CREAMY CHEESE POTATOES

This is a great way to make potatoes into a meal in their own right. Serve with grilled tomatoes for extra colour and flavour.

Ingredients
900g/2 lbs potatoes
2 cloves garlic, crushed
25g/1 oz butter
225g/8 oz strong Welsh cheddar cheese, grated
275ml/½ pint milk
275ml/½ pint double cream
1 tablespoon chopped parsley
salt and pepper

Method
- Peel the potatoes and slice them very thinly. Place in cold water, and when ready to use them, drain and pat them dry.

- Use the butter to grease a 25.5cm/10" gratin dish or ovenproof dish.

- Sprinkle the garlic in the bottom of the dish, then place a layer of potatoes, season with salt and pepper, then sprinkle half the cheese over the potatoes. Place another layer of potatoes on the cheese, and the remaining cheese on top.

- Bring the milk and cream to the boil and pour over the potatoes.

- Bake for 1 hour at 180C/350F/Gas 4.

- Sprinkle with parsley before serving.

APPLE TORTILLA

Ingredients
4 large eggs
1 large red onion, thinly sliced
2 cloves garlic, crushed
225g/8 oz cooked potatoes, cubed
450g/1 lb cooking apples, peeled, cored and finely cubed
1 red or yellow pepper, de-seeded and finely chopped
1 tablespoon chopped parsley
4 tablespoons double cream
110g/4 oz mature cheddar cheese, grated
salt and pepper
olive oil for frying

Method
- Heat the oil in a large frying pan. Fry the onion, garlic and pepper for 3-4 minutes, keeping the crunch in the vegetables.

- Add the potatoes and apples and fry for 2-3 minutes, stirring well.

- Beat the eggs with the cream and season with salt and black pepper.

- Add the chopped parsley and half the cheese and pour into the pan.

- Cook over a low heat until the egg begins to set, then sprinkle over the remaining cheese and place the tortilla under a hot grill.

- It is ready when the cheese has melted and is golden brown.

- To serve: cut into wedges and serve with a green salad.

COCKLE, LAVERBREAD AND LEEK TART

A very Welsh dish indeed, perfect for the cockle season. My earliest memories of childhood food are the ingredients used here – fried bacon, cockles and laverbread, served with home-made bread.

Ingredients
450g/1 lb prepared cockles
225g/8 oz laverbread
2 small leeks, finely chopped
225g/8 oz Welsh lean bacon, finely chopped
50g/2 oz Welsh butter
2-3 tablespoons white wine
25g/1 oz chopped chives and parsley
25g/1 oz oatmeal
450g/1 lb good quality bought puff pastry (or you can make your own)
1 egg, beaten
150ml/¼ pint double cream

Method
- Gently melt the butter in a large frying pan. Add the bacon and leeks and fry for 2-3 minutes.

- Pour in the white wine, bring to the boil and simmer for 2-3 minutes to reduce.

- Add the cockles, laverbread, double cream and oatmeal. Bring to the boil until it reaches a thick consistency. Stir in the parsley and chives and season to taste.

- Divide the pastry in half and roll out one 25.5cm/10" circle and one 28cm/11" circle. Place the smaller circle on a large baking tray and brush the edges with cold water.

- Place the filling on the pastry and cover with the larger circle, making sure the edges are well sealed. Make a slit in the top to allow the steam to escape. Brush the top and sides with the beaten egg.

- Bake at 220C/425F/Gas 7 for about 20 minutes until the pastry is golden brown and crisp.

- Note: you could also make this on an ovenproof plate or a flan tin.

Luxury Welsh Rarebit (p. 13).

Spicy Fish Cakes (p. 17).

Pepper Soup with Organic Yogurt and Soda Bread (p. 26).

Chicken and Rice Tagine (p. 27).

Baked Eggs with Vegetables (p. 34).

Greek Country Salad (p. 38).

Prawns in a Tangy Tomato Sauce (p. 44).

Cockle and Laverbread Filo Parcels (p. 49).

VEGETARIAN DISHES

The days of offering an omelette or a cheese sandwich to vegetarians are long gone, I hope! These ideas should provide some inspiration, and don't forget that you needn't be a vegetarian to enjoy them!

BAKED EGGS WITH VEGETABLES

Ingredients
400g/14 oz tin butter beans
450g/1 lb peeled, chopped tomatoes, fresh or tinned
1 red onion, finely sliced
2 cloves garlic, crushed
1 green pepper, de-seeded and sliced
1 red pepper, de-seeded and sliced
2 tablespoons chopped parsley
4 large eggs
1 tablespoon olive oil
50g/2 oz Welsh butter
50g/2 oz hard Welsh cheese, grated
salt and black pepper

Method
- Heat the oil and butter in a large pan, and fry the onions, garlic and peppers for about 5 minutes.

- Add the tomatoes and drained butter beans, then season well with a little salt and black pepper. Simmer for a further 5 minutes until the mixture is thick. Mix in the parsley.

- Spoon the mixture into a lightly greased ovenproof dish. Make four hollows with the back of a spoon, and break one egg into each hollow.

- Sprinkle over the cheese and bake at 200C/400F/Gas 6 for 15-20 minutes.

- Garnish with parsley and serve hot with crusty bread.

NEW POTATO AND ASPARAGUS SALAD

Potatoes are such a versatile food, and good for us, being full of fibre and carbohydrates. I must say that I love the potatoes that are available from May to July, when they are bursting with flavour. Locally harvested potatoes, from Gower, Pembroke, or even your own garden, are hard to beat.

Ingredients
450g/1 lb Pembroke new potatoes
450g/1 lb asparagus spears
1 red onion, thinly sliced
450g/1 lb cherry tomatoes, halved
2 tablespoons chopped parsley and chives
1 bunch spring onions, thinly sliced

The Dressing
4 tablespoons olive oil
1 tablespoon mustard
1 tablespoon wine vinegar
1 clove garlic, crushed
1 small red chilli, finely chopped

Method
- Wash and scrub the potatoes and cut into quarters. Place them in a large saucepan, cover with water and boil for 15 minutes. Drain and place in a large bowl.

- Steam or microwave the asparagus for 5 minutes.

- When the potatoes have cooled, add the spring onions, red onion, tomatoes, asparagus and herbs.

- To make the dressing: place all the ingredients in a clean jam jar and shake well.

- Pour the dressing onto the vegetables and toss the salad well before serving.

- This salad can be served with cheese cut into cubes, tuna steaks, lamb chops, grilled steak or salmon fillets.

STUFFED CABBAGE LEAVES

Cabbage is a very good source of Vitamin C. There are so many ways of cooking this versatile vegetable. Forget boiling – try this and you'll never go back!

Ingredients
12 large cabbage leaves
150ml/¼ pint vegetable stock

The Stuffing
110g/4 oz chestnut purée
1 small onion, finely chopped
1 clove garlic, crushed
1 tablespoon chopped parsley
110g/4 oz chopped mushrooms
1 teaspoon paprika
50g/2 oz fresh breadcrumbs
2 sticks celery, finely chopped
175g/6 oz ground walnuts
50g/2 oz butter
2 tablespoons brandy
salt and pepper

Method
- In a large pan, melt the butter and fry the onion, celery, mushrooms and garlic for 2-3 minutes.

- Mix in the chestnut purée, breadcrumbs, parsley, walnuts and brandy, and season to taste.

- To prepare the cabbage leaves: blanch them for 1-2 minutes in boiling water, then cut out the centre rib of each leaf.

- Fill each leaf with the stuffing and arrange with the seam side down in a lightly oiled ovenproof dish. Pour over the stock, cover and bake for 15-20 minutes at 180C/350F/Gas 4.

- Serve garnished with lemon slices and mint leaves.

SAVOURY VEGETABLE PIE

*This pie is ideal for vegetarians but, I must admit, I enjoy it very much too –
crunchy vegetables in a tasty white sauce, with a cheese crust pastry to top it
off. Mouthwatering!*

Ingredients
2 large onions
2 carrots
2 large potatoes
3 leeks
225g/8 oz broccoli
2 cloves garlic, crushed
50g/2 oz butter
50g/2 oz plain flour
1 teaspoon mixed herbs
salt and pepper

The Pastry
110g/4 oz strong plain flour
110g/4 oz self-raising flour
110g/4 oz butter
50g/2 oz Welsh cheddar cheese, grated
1 tablespoon chopped parsley

Method

- To make the filling: clean and chop all the vegetables, slice the leeks and cut the broccoli into small florets.

- Place the onions, carrots and potatoes in a large saucepan, cover with cold water and bring to the boil. Simmer for 15 minutes, add the leeks and broccoli and cook for a further 5 minutes.

- Blend the butter and flour together and gradually add to the vegetables. This will thicken to make a lovely sauce.

- Season and add the herbs. Pour into a large pie dish and leave to cool.

- To make the pastry: place the flour in a bowl, and rub in the butter to resemble fine breadcrumbs.

- Add the cheese and parsley then mix to a firm but soft dough with a little cold water.

- Roll out the pastry and use it to cover the vegetables in the dish.

- Brush with beaten egg and bake at 200C/400F/Gas 6 for 15 minutes until the pastry is golden brown.

GREEK COUNTRY SALAD

Greek cookery has much in common with that of other countries of Mediterranean climate. Herbs are used liberally, oregano and basil being the favourites. Olives and olive oil are also essential ingredients. While on holiday in Greece, I thoroughly enjoyed their salads.

Ingredients
3 large tomatoes, sliced
2 tablespoons olive oil
1 tablespoon lemon juice
1 clove garlic, crushed
50g/2 oz pitted green olives
50g/2 oz pitted black olives
110g/4 oz feta cheese, diced
1 red pepper, de-seeded and sliced
1 cos lettuce, washed and drained
1 small jar pepperonata
salt and freshly ground black pepper
fresh oregano leaves

Method
- To make the dressing: whisk the lemon juice, olive oil, salt, pepper and garlic together, or blend them in a food processor.

- Finely shred the lettuce leaves and divide between four small plates. Arrange the sliced tomatoes, red pepper, pepperonata and the black and green olives on top of the lettuce.

- Place the feta cheese in the middle of each salad. Drizzle over the dressing.

- Note: pepperonata are small whole peppers in brine. They can be bought in jars or bottles from delicatessen shops and most supermarkets.

VEGETABLE LASAGNE WITH LEEKS AND LENTILS

Lasagne is a favourite of mine, especially when it has a really tasty sauce, and plenty of it!

Ingredients
450g/1 lb fresh lasagne
450g/1 lb leeks, finely chopped
450g/1 lb carrots, diced
225g/8 oz mushrooms, sliced
2 cloves garlic, crushed
450g/1 lb chopped tomatoes
110g/4 oz red lentils
110g/4 oz Welsh cheddar cheese, grated
1 glass white wine
1 tablespoon shogu sauce
1 teaspoon oregano and marjoram
1 tablespoon olive oil

The Sauce
570ml/1 pint milk
50g/2 oz Welsh butter
50g/2 oz plain flour
salt and pepper

Method
- Heat the oil in a large pan and gently fry the leeks, carrots, mushrooms and garlic for 3-4 minutes.

- Add the lentils, tomatoes, herbs and shogu sauce. Cover and cook for a further 5 minutes, then add the wine and season to taste.

- To make the white sauce: place all the ingredients in a saucepan, gently bring to the boil, stirring all the time until you have a lovely, smooth white sauce. Season with salt and pepper.

- To cook the lasagne: cook in a pan of boiling water with a little olive oil for 5 minutes. Remove on to a tea towel to drain.

- To assemble the lasagne: grease a 725ml/1½ pint lasagne dish with a little oil. Place some of the filling in the bottom, add a layer of lasagne and a layer of white sauce. Repeat this pattern until the dish is full, finishing with the white sauce.

- Sprinkle with grated cheese and cook at 180C/350F/Gas 4 for 20-30 minutes.

- Note: if using dried lasagne, 225g/8 oz will be ample.

POTATO, CHEESE AND CABBAGE CAKES

This recipe is great for vegetarians, and is a clever way of getting children to eat cabbage! You could also make them into smaller cakes and use them in a buffet.

Ingredients
900g/2 lb potatoes
1 small Savoy cabbage
225g/8 oz Welsh cheddar cheese
1/2 teaspoon grated nutmeg
110g/4 oz butter
150ml/¼ pint double cream or natural yogurt
110g/4 oz fine oatmeal
4 tablespoons olive oil
salt and pepper to taste

Method
- Scrub the potatoes until clean, cut them in half and place in a saucepan. Cover with water, bring to the boil and cook for about 15 minutes until the potatoes are cooked. Drain and mash well.

- Add the cheese, butter, cream or yogurt, salt and pepper to the potatoes and mix well.

- Remove any damaged leaves from the cabbage, cut in half and remove the centre stalk. Shred the cabbage thinly, place in a colander and steam over hot water for 2-3 minutes.

- Add the cabbage to the potato and mix well.

- Divide the mixture into eight and mould into round cakes. Toss them in the oatmeal.

- Heat the oil in a large frying pan and fry the cakes for 2-3 minutes on both sides until golden brown.

- To serve: garnish with parsley and serve with salad or seasonal vegetables.

FISH
AND SEAFOOD

As a country surrounded on three sides by sea, we Welsh are spoilt for choice when it comes to fish and seafood dishes. From the exotic to the everyday, whenever you buy it, you can make something delicious for even the fussiest eater. Be adventurous and try something new!

MOC MORGAN PAN FRIED TROUT

I have named this dish after Moc Morgan, Heno's resident fishing expert. The reason for this is that when we were out on location in Cardigan some time ago, he brought me freshly caught trout, and challenged me to cook it there and then! This is the result. Trout producers in Wales have now formed the Welsh Trout Association, to ensure that supply meets demand as more fish are sold into supermarkets. How lovely to have Welsh trout available all year round and produced to such a high quality.

Ingredients
2 350g/12 oz trout, cleaned and prepared
1 tablespoon olive oil
25g/1 oz Welsh butter
freshly ground black pepper

The Sauce
2 tablespoons olive oil
1 red pepper, de-seeded and thinly sliced
1 green pepper, de-seeded and thinly sliced
2 cloves garlic, crushed
1 red chilli, de-seeded and sliced
1 red onion, thinly sliced
rind and juice of 1 lemon
2 tablespoons Thai fish sauce
150ml/¼ pint white wine
1 tablespoon chopped parsley and coriander

Method
- Using a large frying pan, heat the oil and butter and fry the trout for about 4 minutes each side. Remove from the pan and keep warm.

- Heat some more oil in the pan and cook the prepared onion, peppers, garlic and chilli for 2-3 minutes, keeping the crunch in them.

- Add the Thai fish sauce and wine, bring to the boil and simmer for 2-3 minutes.

- Add the grated lemon rind and lemon juice. Season to taste.

- To serve: place the fish on two warm plates and spoon the sauce over them.

- Garnish with the parsley and coriander.

STUFFED BAKED COD

Fish is very good for us as well as tasting wonderful. There is a huge variety of white-fleshed fish available, and in this recipe I use cod, which is very easy to digest. You could also use monkfish, halibut, hake or your particular favourite of this kind of fish.

Ingredients
900g/2 lbs skinned fillet of cod cut into 4 pieces
rind of 2 lemons
1 glass of white wine
110g/4 oz white breadcrumbs
2 cloves garlic, crushed
2 tablespoons chopped parsley
1 tablespoon fresh thyme, chopped
75g/3 oz butter, melted
225g/8 oz Carmarthen ham
3 shallots, chopped
salt and pepper

The Sauce
570ml/1 pint tomato Frito (sieved tomatoes with onion and garlic)
1 red pepper, de-seeded and diced small
1 yellow pepper, de-seeded and diced small
1 orange pepper, de-seeded and diced small
1 red onion, finely chopped
2 tablespoons olive oil

Method
- To prepare the stuffing: mix together the breadcrumbs, garlic, parsley, thyme, seasoning and lemon rind, and bind with the melted butter.
- Lay two fillets of cod, skin side down, on a board. Divide the stuffing between the two fillets, then lay the other two fillets on the stuffing.
- Wrap the Carmarthen ham around each fish parcel, making sure the fish is completely covered. Tie at intervals with string, or use thin skewers.
- Place the fish on a baking tray, pour in the wine, cover with foil and cook at 200C/ 400F/Gas 6 for 20 minutes.
- To make the sauce: heat the oil in a pan and gently fry the chopped peppers and onion for 2-3 minutes without losing texture. Pour in the tomato Frito and any liquid left from the fish and bring to the boil.
- Serve with the cod, garnish with lemon and thyme.

PRAWNS IN A TANGY TOMATO SAUCE

Ingredients
225g/8 oz giant tiger prawns, cooked
175g/6 oz shallots, chopped
2 cloves garlic, crushed
50g/2 oz lean smoked bacon
400g/14 oz tin chopped tomatoes
150ml/¼ pint dry white wine
juice of 1 lemon
a few drops Tabasco sauce
150ml/¼ pint tomato Frito
2 teaspoons caster sugar
2 tablespoons chopped basil
salt and pepper

Method
- Heat a non-stick pan and gently fry the bacon and shallots.

- Add the garlic, tomatoes, tomato Frito, wine, Tabasco sauce and sugar. Bring to the boil and simmer for 2-3 minutes.

- Add the lemon juice and seasoning and stir in the cooked prawns. If using raw prawns, pour boiling water over them and watch them change colour from grey to pink, and from translucent to opaque.

- Stir in the chopped basil and heat through.

SALMON STIR-FRY WITH BAKED POTATO CHIPS

As a child, I loved the treat of fish and chips on a Saturday night. In these days of cutting down on our fat intake, I have given the traditional dish a lower-calorie twist.

Ingredients
400g/14 oz salmon, fresh or tinned
2 cloves garlic, crushed
110g/4 oz baby corn, cut in half lengthways
4 spring onions, sliced
1 red pepper, de-seeded and sliced
110g/4 oz mangetout
110g/4 oz button mushrooms
110g/4 oz beansprouts
juice and rind of 1 orange
1 tablespoon olive oil
1 teaspoon minced root ginger
1 tablespoon soy sauce
1 tablespoon tomato purée
4 large potatoes, microwaved for 8 minutes
2 teaspoons cornflour

Method
- Heat the oil in a wok or large frying pan, add the ginger, soy sauce and garlic and quickly cook for 1 minute.

- Stir in the baby corn, pepper, mushrooms and mangetout and cook for 3-4 minutes, stirring constantly.

- Add the spring onions and beansprouts and stir-fry for 2-3 minutes.

- Mix the cornflour into the orange juice, add the tomato purée and pour into the pan, stirring through the vegetables.

- Flake the salmon carefully (drain if using tinned, grill and cool if using fresh) and toss into the vegetables with the orange rind.

- Heat a grill pan or a non-stick pan and pour in 2-3 tablespoons light olive oil. Cut the jacket potatoes into chips and quickly fry in the hot oil. Drain on kitchen paper, season, and carefully toss into the salmon and vegetables.

- Garnish with plenty of parsley or chives.

COD STEAK WITH YOGURT

Ingredients
4 portions 175g/6 oz cod steaks
110g/4 oz white breadcrumbs
1 tablespoon chopped parsley and chives
2 shallots, chopped
25g/1 oz butter
425ml/¾ pint organic Greek-type yogurt
a little salt

Method
- Place the cod steaks in an ovenproof dish.

- To make the topping: melt the butter in a saucepan and gently fry the chopped shallots. Mix in the breadcrumbs and herbs.

- Scatter the topping over the fish, pour in the yogurt and bake in a pre-heated oven at 180C/350F/Gas 4 for about 15 minutes until the topping is golden brown and the fish is nice and flaky.

- Serve with buttered carrots and garlic mashed potatoes.

PAN GRILLED SALMON WITH WHITE WINE SAUCE

Ingredients
700g/1½ lb salmon fillet
1 tablespoon olive oil
25g/1 oz butter

The Sauce
1 large tomato, skinned and de-seeded
1 small red onion, finely chopped
1 tablespoon chopped fresh chives
25g/1 oz butter
275ml/½ pint white wine
275ml/½ pint fish stock
200ml/6 fl oz double cream
1 teaspoon caster sugar
freshly ground black pepper
lemon slices and watercress to garnish

Method
- To make the sauce: melt the butter in a saucepan, add the onion and cook for 2-3 minutes without browning.

- Add the wine and stock and boil rapidly to reduce by three-quarters.

- Pour in the double cream and boil until the sauce coats the back of a spoon. Add the chopped tomato, sugar and chives, and keep warm.

- To pan grill the salmon: melt the butter and oil in a grill pan. Place the salmon flesh side down and cook for 2-3 minutes.

- Using a palette knife or a fish slice, turn the salmon over and cook for a further minute.

- Serve the salmon on a bed of minted mashed potatoes and pour the sauce around.

- Sprinkle the salmon with freshly ground black pepper and garnish with lemon slices and watercress.

- Note: you could also make this recipe with cod, hake, haddock, or even trout.

COCKLE AND LAVERBREAD FILO PARCELS

These little parcels are ideal for a buffet or as a starter. Filo pastry is available in most good food shops.

Ingredients
8 sheets filo pastry
225g/8 oz prepared cockles
225g/8 oz laverbread
1 small leek, finely chopped
2 tablespoons Greek-style natural yogurt
50g/2 oz Welsh butter, melted
salt and pepper to taste

Method
- Divide each sheet of filo into four squares, brush each layer with butter and arrange on top of each other.

- Mix together the cockles, laverbread, leek, yogurt, salt and pepper.

- Divide the mixture between the eight prepared pastry squares. Bring each corner up and pinch together to make a little parcel. Brush each one with the remaining butter.

- Place on a baking tray and cook at 200C/400F/Gas 6 for 10-15 minutes.

- To serve: two parcels per person with a garnish of your choice.

MUSSELS AND LEEKS WITH WHITE WINE SAUCE

Mussels, those small shellfish that are so plentiful in Wales, are an acquired taste. They should always be eaten as fresh as possible. Always scrub them well before cooking. Some people eat the beard, which is the slightly gristly ring around the mussel, but this can be pulled away with a fork before serving. Discard any open mussels that do not close when lightly tapped.

Ingredients
900g/2 lb mussels
450g/1 lb leeks, finely chopped
150ml/¼ pint water
150ml/¼ pint white wine
50g/2 oz butter, softened
150ml/¼ pint double cream
25g/1 oz plain flour
chopped parsley
ground black pepper

Method
- Place the leeks in a saucepan. Add the cleaned mussels then pour in the wine and water. Cover and cook over a high heat for 3-4 minutes, shaking the pan until the mussels have opened. Drain the mussels into a colander.

- Pour the liquid back into a saucepan with the leeks. Mix the butter and flour together. Gradually whisk into the reduced liquid.

- Bring to the boil, pour in the cream and boil for a further 1-2 minutes.

- Season to taste, and add the chopped parsley. Add the mussels to the sauce.

- Serve in soup bowls with crusty bread.

DRESSED CRAB IN SHELL

Crabs are in season from May to September. Good crabs are heavy for their size, their claws containing most of the white meat. For four people allow a 900g/2 lb crab. Crabs are usually sold ready dressed, but if alive, boil them gently in salted water allowing 15 minutes per 450g/1 lb. Cool in the liquid before taking out.

To dress crab

- Remove the big claws and set aside. Twist off the small claws, at the same time removing the crab's body or undershell, and set aside.

- Take out and throw away the following parts: the small sac lying in the top of the big shell; any green matter in the big shell; the spongy fingers or lungs lying around the big shell.

- Using a crab pick, remove the meat, which is the brown creamy part lying around the sides of the big shell.

- Holding the shell firmly, break down the sides. The shell should now be washed well and dried.

- Cut the body of the crab in two and remove all the white meat with a crab pick or skewer and place in a bowl.

- Crack the big claws and and remove all the meat. Collect all the white meat together and put to one side.

- Cream the brown meat together and season with salt, pepper and mustard. If the mixture is dry, add 1 tablespoon cream. The brown meat should be arranged across the middle of the shell with the white meat on either side.

- When serving crab cold, you can decorate it with sieved hard-boiled eggs and chopped parsley.

- Place the shell in the middle of a serving plate, arrange lettuce leaves around it and add the claws for decoration.

- Serve with tartare sauce or garlic mayonnaise and brown bread or toast – delicious!

STUFFED BAKED SEWIN

Perhaps the best-kept secret in Wales, sewin is a beautifully delicate fish from the trout family. Years ago, when all our rivers were clean, my Uncle Willie from Felindre would fish all night. He would often lose track of time, and then have to run quickly home with his catch to Auntie Getta and his brothers. Then he'd be off to an early shift at Graig Ola Merthyr, Pontardulais! The fish would be fried or poached for lunch that very day. Sewin can be poached, grilled, fried or stuffed and baked, depending on its size.

Ingredients
900g/2 lb whole sewin
50g/2 oz butter

The Stuffing
50g/2 oz butter
3 shallots, chopped
110g/4 oz mushrooms, chopped
1 tablespoon parsley, chopped
1 tablespoon dill, chopped
75g/3 oz white breadcrumbs

The Sauce
150ml/¼ pint sour cream or double
    cream
1 teaspoon caster sugar
rind and juice of 1 lemon
salt and pepper

Method
- Ask your fishmonger to bone the fish, leaving the head and tail on.

- To make the stuffing: melt the butter in a saucepan and fry the shallots and mushrooms for 2-3 minutes. Add the breadcrumbs, parsley and dill and mix well.

- Place the stuffing in the cavity of the fish and place in a buttered baking dish.

- Pour some melted butter over it and cook at 180C/350F/Gas 4 for 25-30 minutes. You could cook it in foil and reserve all the juices.

- To make the sauce: combine all the sauce ingredients and fish juices, gently heat in a saucepan but do not boil.

- Remove the sewin on to a serving plate, pour the sauce over it and garnish with lemon and parsley.

POULTRY
AND GAME

There is an increasing number of organic producers in Wales rearing all kinds of birds. While many, like pheasant, are best tasted fresh in season, others are available all year round, and can make a tasty addition to any bird-lover's table. You may like to experiment at Christmas as well.

SPICED CHICKEN WITH ORANGE
AND GRAPE SAUCE

Trying to lose weight, or eating healthily, can be boring unless you add colour and spice to your food. This is one such dish that the whole family will love.

Ingredients
4 chicken breasts, skin removed
175g/6 oz shallots, chopped
175g/6 oz seedless green grapes
2 oranges, segmented
2 tablespoons olive oil
2 cloves garlic, crushed
1 teaspoon ground coriander
1 teaspoon ground turmeric
275ml/½ pint chicken stock
150ml/¼ pint organic natural yogurt
salt and pepper to taste

Method
- Heat the oil in a large pan, add the chicken portions and cook until brown on both sides.

- Remove the chicken on to a plate, and fry the shallots, garlic and spices for 2-3 minutes.

- Place the chicken back in the pan and pour in the stock. Bring to the boil, cover and simmer for about 15 minutes until cooked.

- Stir in the grapes, orange segments and yogurt, and gently heat through. Taste and adjust the seasoning.

- Serve with cooked wild rice and steamed broccoli.

DUCK BREASTS WITH APPLE AND WELSH HONEY SAUCE

This recipe makes a lovely supper dish. I think duck breasts cooked in this way are a nicer meal than cooking a whole duck.

Ingredients
4 duck breast fillets
3 tablespoons clear Welsh honey
225g/8 oz red plums, stones removed
150ml/¼ pint wine
150ml/¼ pint apple juice
salt and pepper

Method
- Using a sharp knife, score the skin of the duck. Rub with salt and pepper.

- Pre-heat a heavy, heatproof pan. Place the breasts, skin side down, over a medium heat.

- Cook for 7-8 minutes, turn the duck and cook for a further 3-4 minutes. The duck should be pink, but if you prefer it well done, allow more time.

- Remove the duck on to a serving plate and keep warm.

- To make the sauce: pour all the excess fat from the pan away. Add the wine, honey, apple juice and plums and bring to the boil to reduce slightly.

- Garnish with watercress and serve with a medley of stir-fried vegetables and diced potatoes cooked in butter and oil.

SPICY LEMON CHICKEN

Ingredients
700g/1½ lbs chicken portions
juice of 4 lemons
8 cloves garlic
2 small red chillis, finely chopped
1 tablespoon honey
2 tablespoons Thai curry paste
4 tablespoons chopped parsley
salt and pepper

Method
- Place the chicken portions in a large shallow roasting tin.
- Pour the lemon juice into a basin, add the chillis, garlic cloves, curry paste and honey, and blend until smooth.
- Pour over the chicken and leave to marinade for 2 hours, turning once or twice.
- Cook at 200C/400F/Gas 6 for 30-40 minutes until golden brown.
- Note: this recipe is ideal for a barbecue, since you can prepare it early and adjust the cooking time according to the intensity of the barbecue.

BRAISED PIGEON

Pigeons tend to be rather dry birds, so braising is the best way to cook them. Choose young wood pigeons, which should cook in about 1½ hours.

Ingredients
4 young oven-ready wood pigeons
2 tablespoons olive oil
225g/8 oz carrots, chopped
225g/8 oz celery, chopped
225g/8 oz shallots, cleaned whole
6 rashers streaky bacon, chopped
725ml/1½ pints chicken stock
275ml/½ pint dry white wine
large bunch of parsley and thyme
salt and pepper

Method
- Wash the pigeons under cold water and pat dry.

- Place parsley and thyme inside each one and tie the legs.

- Heat the oil in a large pan and fry the pigeons to seal them all over. Place in a large casserole dish.

- Fry the bacon, celery and shallots for 2-3 minutes and add to the casserole with the carrots and seasoning.

- Pour the wine and stock into the frying pan to de-glaze all the lovely juices; bring to the boil and pour into the casserole. Cover and cook at 180C/ 350F/Gas 4 for about 1½ hours.

- The liquid can be thickened with a little blended cornflour.

- Serve from the casserole, garnished with plenty of parsley.

RABBIT IN A BUTTERY WINE SAUCE

Ingredients
1 whole rabbit, cleaned and cut into portions
50g/2 oz butter
1 tablespoon olive oil
450g/1 lb button onions
225g/8 oz button mushrooms
275ml/½ pint white wine
150ml/¼ pint crème fraîche
2 tablespoons parsley, chopped
salt and pepper

Method
- Heat the butter and oil in a large frying pan and fry the rabbit portions on both sides until golden brown. Add the onions and mushrooms.

- Pour in the wine, cover and simmer for 15-20 minutes until the rabbit is cooked.

- Remove the rabbit on to a serving plate. Add the crème fraîche to the sauce and heat until it blends. Pour over the rabbit.

- Garnish with parsley and serve with vegetables of your choice.

CHICKEN IN CIDER AND CREAM SAUCE

Ingredients
4 chicken breasts
225g/8 oz button onions, chopped
2 hot red chillis, finely chopped
1 teaspoon mustard
2 cloves garlic, crushed
225g/8 oz rindless smoked bacon, chopped
225g/8 oz button mushrooms, sliced
2 tablespoons olive oil
50g/2 oz butter
150ml/¼ pint dry cider
150ml/¼ pint chicken stock
150ml/¼ pint double cream or crème fraîche
salt and black pepper

Method
- Heat the oil and butter in a pan and fry the chicken portions until brown on both sides, then remove onto a plate.

- To the pan, add the bacon, mustard, garlic, chillis and onions. Fry until the bacon is crisp.

- Add the mushrooms, then pour in the stock and cider and bring to the boil.

- Return the chicken to the pan, cover and cook for a further 15 minutes. Season to taste and pour in the crème fraîche.

- Serve with pan-grilled peppers, red onions and slices of apple.

ORGANIC OSTRICH FILLET STEAKS IN A WINE SAUCE

There are several ostrich farms in Wales now, many of them rearing organic birds. Ostrich meat is very low in fat, and is as easy to prepare as beef. It is usually grilled, but do be careful not to over-cook this tender meat. Many restaurants serve ostrich dishes, and it is becoming more readily available. I am particularly fond of this recipe.

Ingredients
4 ostrich fillets, each about 175g/6 oz in weight
2 tablespoons olive oil
25g/1 oz butter
225g/8 oz button mushrooms
225g/8 oz button onions
225g/8 oz kumquats
2 cloves garlic, crushed
1 red pepper, de-seeded and sliced
350g/12 oz tin of pineapple in its own juice
570ml/1 pint Cwm Deri elderberry wine
2 tablespoons redcurrant jelly
1 tablespoon cornflour
1 tablespoon Demerara sugar
salt and pepper

Method
- Heat the oil and butter in a large pan, making sure it is really hot before you add the steaks. Fry the steaks for about 2 minutes on either side to seal the juices. Remove from the pan on to a plate.

- Fry the mushrooms, onions, garlic and sliced pepper for 2-3 minutes.

- Next pour in the wine, add the pineapple and redcurrant jelly and kumquats, bring to the boil and season with salt and pepper.

- Place the steaks in the sauce with the sugar and simmer for 15-20 minutes. Thicken the sauce with blended cornflour.

- Serve hot, garnished with chopped parsley.

INDIVIDUAL TURKEY ROLLS

This recipe is ideal for one or two people; a joint is too much, therefore turkey steaks are the answer. You could use chicken breasts if you intend inviting a friend to dinner, and the cost is reasonable.

Ingredients
4 turkey steaks
2 tablespoons olive oil
110g/4 oz white breadcrumbs
2 slices bacon, chopped
2 shallots, finely chopped
1 teaspoon mixed herbs
1 tablespoon chopped parsley
275ml/½ pint chicken stock
1 small egg, beaten
salt and pepper
50g/2 oz butter

The Sauce
150ml/¼ pint stock
half a cup red wine
2 tablespoons cranberry sauce

Method
- To make the stuffing: melt the butter in a saucepan and fry the onion and bacon for 2-3 minutes. Mix in the breadcrumbs, parsley, mixed herbs, seasoning and the egg to bind the stuffing.

- Place the turkey steaks between two sheets of clingfilm. Using a rolling pin, flatten the steaks until thin.

- Divide the stuffing between each steak, roll up and secure with a cocktail stick.

- Heat the oil in a large pan and quickly fry each roll until golden brown. Lift into a large gratin dish or any ovenproof dish. Pour in the stock, cover and cook for about 40-50 minutes at 180C/350F/Gas 4.

- When the turkey rolls are cooked, remove on to a plate and keep warm.

- To make the sauce: use the liquid from the cooking tray. Add the ingredients of the sauce, bring to the boil and thicken with a little blended cornflour. Season to taste.

- Serve hot with vegetables and sauce, or slice them cold with salad.

MEAT

*We are very lucky in Wales to have such a
wide range of quality meat reared by our
farmers. Although the farming industry
has been going through a difficult time, if
the public supports it by buying home-grown
produce, long may it prosper in future.
Keep an eye on the ever-increasing variety
of organic meat available, and don't forget
your local butcher when looking for a really
special cut of meat.*

PEPPERED BEEF AND VEGETABLE PIE WITH POTATO AND CELERIAC TOPPING

Savoury pies are very popular for family meals. They can be prepared in advance and are very convenient. You have a complete meal in one dish, full of flavour and very nutritious. There are many toppings to use: pastry, potato and parsnip, croûtons and savoury scone dough. This is a firm favourite in our house.

Ingredients
700g/1½ lbs quality Welsh
   stewing beef
50g/2 oz cornflour
1 tablespoon olive oil
3 cloves garlic, crushed
2 tablespoons tomato paste
275ml/½ pint red wine
275ml/½ pint beef stock
2 tablespoons redcurrant jelly
1 tablespoon coarsely ground black pepper
110g/4 oz button mushrooms
225g/8 oz baby carrots
sprig of thyme

Topping
900g/2 lbs Welsh potatoes
450g/1 lb celeriac
50g/2 oz butter
2 tablespoons chopped parsley
salt and pepper

Method
- Clean and prepare all the vegetables.

- Cut the meat into 5cm/2" pieces, removing any excess fat. Then toss the meat in the cornflour and season.

- Heat the oil in a large pan and fry the meat until it is brown all over, sealing the meat to give the pie a rich flavour.

- Add the onions, garlic, redcurrant jelly, tomato paste and thyme and cook for 3-4 minutes. At this point pour in the wine and stock, bring to the boil, reduce the heat and simmer for 15 minutes.

- Add the carrots and mushrooms and cook for another 15 minutes. The sauce should be glossy and should coat the back of a spoon. Pour the mixture into a deep pie dish.

- To make the topping: boil the potatoes and celeriac together for 15 minutes, drain, mash, then add the butter, parsley and seasoning.

- Pipe the potato and celeriac over the meat, and cook for 30 minutes at 200C/400F/Gas 6, until the topping is golden brown.

- Note: you could also use venison, lamb or chicken to make this pie.

STUFFED LEG OF WELSH LAMB WITH ROSEMARY

Ingredients
1.35kg/3 lb boned leg of Welsh lamb
450g/1 lb shallots
1 clove garlic
1 tablespoon cooking oil
a generous bunch of rosemary

The Stuffing
110g/4 oz finely chopped onion
110g/4 oz finely chopped celery
50g/2 oz ready-to-eat apricots, cut into small pieces
50g/2 oz chopped walnuts
110g/4 oz white breadcrumbs
2 tablespoons chopped parsley and thyme
1 egg

The Sauce
275ml/½ pint stock
275ml/½ pint red wine
2 tablespoons redcurrant jelly
2 tablespoons mint jelly
1 tablespoon cornflour
salt and pepper

Method

- First, make the stuffing. Melt the butter in a pan, add the onion, celery and garlic and cook for 2-3 minutes. Add to this the breadcrumbs, with the parsley, thyme, apricots and walnuts. Season to taste and bind together with the egg.

- Stuff the bone cavity of the lamb with the mixture, then secure with string or skewers.

- To prepare the lamb: heat the cooking oil in a roasting tin and quickly brown the lamb on both sides. Place the rosemary under the lamb and add the shallots and garlic to the tin. Sprinkle over a little salt and roast for 1½ hours at 200C/400F/Gas 6. Baste from time to time.

- When the lamb is pink, it is ready. Remove onto a carving plate with the shallots and keep warm.

- To make the sauce: pour away any excess fat from the roasting tin, keeping the beautifully flavoured sediment. Pour in the stock, wine and jellies. Bring to the boil and thicken slightly with blended cornflour. Season to taste, and serve with the lamb and vegetables for a feast!

PORK, CHICKEN AND APRICOT TERRINE

Terrines or meat loaves are very useful to have prepared and ready to use at holiday times. This one was made with Easter in mind, so make it a week in advance and hope that the weather allows you to arrange a picnic!

Ingredients
450g/1 lb minced Welsh pork
2 large chicken breasts, minced
450g/1 lb streaky bacon rashers
110g/4 oz ready-to-eat apricots, finely chopped
75ml/3 fl oz brandy
50g/2 oz butter
4 shallots, finely chopped
2 tablespoons chopped parsley
1 tablespoon chopped fresh thyme
2 cloves garlic, crushed
175g/6 oz fresh white breadcrumbs
2 eggs
1 tablespoon drained canned peppercorns
1 teaspoon coriander
1 teaspoon cumin
salt and pepper

Method
- Finely chop 4 slices of the bacon and add to the minced pork and minced chicken breasts.

- Melt the butter in a pan and gently fry the shallots and garlic until soft.

- Mix together with the pork, chicken, chopped bacon, apricots, onion, parsley, breadcrumbs, eggs and peppercorns. Pour in the brandy, add the spices and mix well. Season to taste.

- Line a 9" x 3" or 700g/1½ lb loaf tin with the remaining bacon, keeping some for the top.

- Spoon the mixture into the tin and even out with a spoon or knife. Top with the reserved bacon and cover with foil.

- Place on a baking tray with a little water and cook for about an hour at 180C/350F/Gas 4.

- Serve cold in thick slices with mango chutney, salad and new potatoes or rice salad.

PAN FRIED WELSH PORK WITH JUICY PLUMS

This recipe is a delicious combination of tender pork fillets and juicy red plums. It's perfect for busy people who have very little time to devote to cooking.

Ingredients
450g/1 lb Welsh pork fillet
25g/1 oz butter
1 tablespoon olive oil
225g/8 oz fresh red plums, halved and stoned
275ml/½ pint red wine
2 tablespoons cornflour
a generous bunch spring onions, chopped
1 tablespoon freshly chopped parsley and thyme
2 tablespoons Demerara sugar
few drops Tabasco sauce
salt and pepper

Method
- Slice the pork into 1.5cm/½ inch pieces and toss in the cornflour, seasoned to taste.
- Heat the butter and oil in a pan, add the pork and quickly fry until brown all over.
- Add the plums, red wine and Tabasco sauce, bring to the boil, cover and simmer for 10-15 minutes.
- Add the chopped spring onions and parsley and thyme. Taste for seasoning.
- Serve with green vegetables.

WELSH BLACK FILLET OF BEEF WITH MUSHROOMS, GARLIC AND CREAM SAUCE

This is a perfect recipe for a special quick supper. Beef is my favourite meat, especially Welsh Black beef. With the fillet, there is no waste, so expensive though it may be, it is worth it for the beautiful succulent flavour.

Ingredients
2 175g/6 oz Welsh Black fillet
  steaks
2 teaspoons creamed horseradish
  sauce
1 tablespoon chopped mint
2 tablespoons olive oil

The Sauce
110g/4 oz mushrooms, chopped
2 cloves garlic, crushed
2 shallots, finely chopped
275ml/½ pint double cream
150ml/¼ pint white wine
ground black pepper and salt
    to taste

Method
- Cut a pocket in each fillet, then spread the horseradish and mint inside each pocket.

- Heat the olive oil in a grill pan until very hot and cook the steaks for the required time. Set aside and keep warm while making the sauce.

- To the pan, add the mushrooms, garlic and chopped shallots and fry for 2-3 minutes. Pour in the wine to de-glaze the flavour in the pan.

- Simmer for 2-3 minutes then pour in the cream and gently bring to the boil. Season to taste.

- To serve: place on a serving plate with grilled tomatoes and mashed potato with celeriac. Pour the sauce around and garnish with parsley and chives.

CARMARTHEN SAUSAGE AND LAVERBREAD SAUCE

Carmarthen Ham is popular throughout Wales, and indeed in England too. It is a delicious home-dried and cured ham. It can be used in savoury dishes or with fruit. This recipe is my creation of a 'Carmarthen sausage'.

Ingredients
350g/12 oz potatoes
225g/8 oz parsnips
225g/8 oz celeriac
110g/4 oz Carmarthen ham,
   chopped
2 tablespoons parsley, chopped
¼ teaspoon ground nutmeg
1 small egg
50g/2 oz mature farmhouse
   cheese, grated

Laverbread Sauce
225g/8 oz laverbread
275ml/½ pint organic crème fraîche
2 drops Tabasco sauce

Coating
225g/8 oz white breadcrumbs
2 large eggs
150ml/¼ pint milk
4 tablespoons oil for frying

Method
- Peel the vegetables and cut into large pieces. Place in a saucepan, cover with cold water, bring to the boil and simmer for 15 minutes until cooked. Drain the vegetables and mash well.

- Add the ham, parsley, nutmeg, cheese and beaten egg to the mash. Mix well and leave to cool.

- Roll into a long sausage and divide into 8 smaller sausages.

- To coat: beat the eggs and milk together. Dip each sausage in the mixture and toss in the breadcrumbs.

- Heat the oil and fry the sausages quickly, turning them as they cook until they are golden brown.

- Lift on to kitchen paper to drain away the fat.

- To make the sauce: place the laverbread and crème fraîche in a saucepan and bring to the boil slowly. Season with Tabasco sauce and salt and pepper. Serve two sausages per person with the sauce poured around them.

- Note: the sausages are easier to cook if you chill them first.

EGG AND CRISP BACON SALAD WITH CROÛTONS

Ingredients
4 eggs
4 rashers streaky bacon
1 head frisée lettuce

The Dressing
2 tablespoons walnut oil
1 tablespoon olive oil
1 tablespoon white wine vinegar
1 teaspoon Welsh wholegrain mustard
ground black pepper

The Croûtons
2 thick slices white bread
50g/2 oz salted Welsh butter

Method
- Place the eggs in a saucepan and cover with cold water. Bring to the boil and cook for 10 minutes. Run cold water over the eggs to prevent further cooking. Remove the shells and put the eggs to one side.

- Grill or fry the bacon until crisp, then cut into bite-size pieces.

- Cut the crusts off the bread and cut into small cubes. Melt the butter in a frying pan and fry the bread pieces until crisp on both sides. Be **very** careful not to burn them – it's easily done!

- To assemble the meal: arrange the lettuce leaves on a serving plate. Cut the eggs in half and sprinkle the bacon and croutons over them.

- Mix all the dressing ingredients together and drizzle over the salad.

- This is ideal as a starter or a snack.

STUFFED FILLET OF WELSH BEEF

Although we don't always have hot summers in Wales, we usually try to squeeze in a few barbecues during the holiday period. This is a luxurious alternative to sausages and burgers!

Ingredients
4 thick-cut fillets of Welsh beef
4 rashers of bacon
50g/2 oz butter
4 shallots, chopped
50g/2 oz finely chopped mushrooms
1 clove garlic, crushed
50g/2 oz white breadcrumbs
rind of 1 lemon

Method
- To make the stuffing: melt the butter in a pan and gently fry the shallots.

- Add the mushrooms and garlic and fry for 1-2 minutes.

- Add the lemon rind and breadcrumbs and mix well.

- Cut a pocket in the side of each steak and fill with stuffing.

- Wrap each steak in a rasher of bacon and secure with cocktail sticks.

- Cook on a hot barbecue for 2-3 minutes each side.

- Serve with crusty bread and as many different salads as you like!

ENA'S FAGGOTS

My mother used to make faggots every week and she would use the whole of the pig's fry. However, I only use the liver and the heart, and I have to say that faggots and peas are one of my favourites for lunch. They even taste good eaten cold.

Ingredients
450g/1 lb pig's liver
350g/12 oz pig's heart
225g/8 oz breadcrumbs
225g/8 oz cooking apples, cored and peeled
2 onions, roughly chopped
225g/8 oz lean bacon
2 teaspoons mixed herbs
a pig's apron or caul
salt and pepper

Method
- Place the apron or caul in boiling water to soak.

- Mince the liver, heart, bacon, onions and apples.

- Place the mixture in a large bowl. Add the breadcrumbs, mixed herbs and seasoning.

- Mix together well, then using an ice-cream scoop mould the faggots and place in a baking tray packed well together.

- Cover the faggots completely with the apron and pour a little water over it all.

- Cook at 190C/375F/Gas 5 for 30-40 minutes.

- Serve with mashed potatoes, gravy and mushy or garden peas.

STUFFED WELSH LAMB CUTLETS

Juicy and tender, Welsh lamb is hard to beat!

Ingredients
900g/2 lb loin of lamb

The Stuffing
1 onion, finely chopped
225g/8 oz white breadcrumbs
50g/2 oz melted butter or oil
rind of 1 orange
225g/8 oz pineapple pieces, chopped
1 tablespoon parsley, chopped
1 teaspoon thyme, chopped
110g/4 oz pork sausagemeat

The Sauce
275ml/½ pint white wine
150ml/¼ pint double cream
1 tablespoon tarragon, chopped
salt and pepper

Method
- Remove the skin and bone off the loin.

- To make the stuffing: place the onion and all the stuffing ingredients in a large bowl and mix well to bind together.

- Place the stuffing down the centre of the loin and roll the meat around the stuffing. Tie with string at 2.5cm/1" intervals. Cut each cutlet between the string.

- Fry gently in hot oil for 3 minutes on each side. Keep warm.

- To make the sauce: pour away any excess fat from the frying pan. Pour in the wine to de-glaze the flavours in the pan. Bring to the boil and simmer for 2-3 minutes.

- Pour in the cream and boil for 1-2 minutes. Season to taste and add the tarragon.

- Serve the cutlets with the sauce, glazed onions and green vegetables.

SPECIAL OCCASIONS

This chapter has been designed to suggest ideas for any special occasion – an engagement, a christening or supper for old friends, for example. Some of the recipes need great care in the preparation; others can be assembled at short notice, provided that you have the ingredients to hand.

OYSTERS IN CHAMPAGNE SAUCE

Oysters in Wales are in season from September to April. They are at their best served chilled and raw as a first course, with lemon juice, Tabasco sauce and black pepper. However, many people prefer them cooked.

Ingredients
16 well-scrubbed oysters in their shells

The Sauce
1 shallot, finely chopped
50g/2 oz butter
175ml/6 fl oz champagne
175ml/6 fl oz stock from oysters (see method below)
1 teaspoon caster sugar
175ml/6 fl oz double cream
1 tablespoon parsley, finely chopped

Method
- Pour some boiling water into a large saucepan. Place a steamer or sieve on top, put in the oysters and steam for 4 minutes.

- Remove the oysters from the pan and open, taking care to reserve the juices for the stock.

- Arrange the oysters on a serving plate, garnish with lemon and pour the champagne sauce around them.

- To make the sauce: melt the butter in a small saucepan and fry the shallot. Then pour in the champagne and oyster juice stock, and boil rapidly until it has reduced by three-quarters.

- Add the sugar and cream, boil for 2-3 minutes until the sauce will coat the back of a spoon. Stir in the parsley and taste for seasoning. Pour around the oysters.

- Note: this sauce can also be used with salmon.

VENISON PÂTÉ AND CUMBERLAND SAUCE

Ingredients
450g/1 lb venison
450g/1 lb minced pork
1 large clove garlic, crushed
1 teaspoon fresh thyme
1 teaspoon allspice
 pinch ground black pepper
3 tablespoons brandy
1 egg
juice and rind of 1 orange
275g/10 oz thinly sliced unsmoked streaky bacon

The Sauce
2 oranges
1 lemon
225g/8 oz redcurrant jelly
3 tablespoons port
1 desertspoon mustard

Method

- Mince the venison and pork and mix well together.

- Add the garlic, thyme, allspice, seasoning, egg, brandy and orange juice and rind. Mix thoroughly.

- Line a 900g/2 lb loaf tin with the bacon and spoon the pâté mixture into the tin. Press down with the back of the spoon.

- Cover the pâté with foil and place it in a roasting tin half-filled with water.

- Place in the oven and cook at 170C/325F/Gas 3 for 1½ hours. Leave the pâté to cool in the tin before turning it out.

- Chill overnight in the fridge.

- To make the sauce: using a rind peeler, pare the rind of the oranges and lemons. Place the rind and juice in a saucepan and add the other ingredients.

- Heat gently until the jelly dissolves and the ingredients are blended smoothly. Simmer for 2-3 minutes.

- To serve: cut the pâté into slices and serve with the sauce and salads of your choice.

THAI GREEN CURRY

This delicious creamy Thai curry is perfect for a dinner party, especially if your guests like the combination of herbs, spices and chillis which makes Thai food so special.

Ingredients
4 skinless chicken fillets
1 red chilli, de-seeded and finely chopped
1 bunch spring onions, sliced
2.5cm/1" root ginger
1 stick lemon grass
2 tablespoons olive oil
225g/8 oz brown cup or oyster mushrooms
1 level tablespoon Thai green curry paste
275ml/½ pint coconut milk
150ml/¼ pint chicken stock
1 tablespoon Thai fish sauce
2 teaspoons soy sauce
2 tablespoons chopped coriander
1 tablespoon mango chutney
1 clove garlic, crushed

Method
- Cut the chicken into bite-size pieces.

- Peel and finely grate the ginger. Cut the lemon grass into large pieces so that you can remove it after cooking.

- Heat the oil in a wok or large frying pan and stir-fry the chicken for 2-3 minutes.

- Add the ginger, mushrooms, lemon grass, curry paste, Thai fish sauce, soy sauce and garlic and cook for 3 minutes.

- Pour in the coconut milk and stock, bring to the boil and simmer for about 4 minutes.

- Add the spring onions and chutney.

- Remove the lemon grass, garnish with coriander and serve with fragrant Thai rice.

SPECIAL SALMON

A whole salmon, beautifully dressed, looks splendid on a buffet table, but it is tricky to serve, and can be quite messy. Why not try my version of poached salmon? Ask your fishmonger to remove the head completely, bone the salmon and remove the skin, leaving the tail intact. This makes it much easier to handle and serve.

Ingredients	Savoury Rice
1 whole salmon about	225g/8 oz long grain rice
1.2 kg/2½ lbs	150ml/¼ pint organic natural yogurt
1 glass white wine	3 tablespoons mayonnaise
2 lemons, cut in slices	50g/2 oz sultanas
juice and rind of 1 lemon	50g/2 oz flaked almonds
cucumber and lemon slices	2 oranges, peeled and segmented
to garnish	2 tablespoons parsley
	salt and pepper

Method

- Place the boned and skinned salmon on a large piece of foil. Open the fish and insert the lemon slices along the length of the salmon. Close the fish and pour the wine and the juice and rind of the other lemon over it.

- Make a secure parcel with the foil, wrapping the salmon thoroughly. Place on a baking tray and bake at 180C/350F/Gas 4 for 15-20 minutes. Leave to cool in the foil, then remove onto a serving plate, gently rolling it over. Add the garnish.

- To prepare the rice: place the rice into a saucepan, cover with boiling water and cook for 10-15 minutes. Drain and run under cold water to separate the grains.

- Mix in the yogurt, mayonnaise, sultanas, almonds, parsley and seasoning. Arrange in a bowl and decorate with orange segments. Serve with the salmon.

- Note: placing the lemon slices inside the fish makes them go soft, like a mousse, and gives the fish an extra infusion of lemon.

STUFFED WELSH LAMB FILLET IN PUFF PASTRY

Ingredients
450g/1 lb Welsh lamb fillet
225g/8 oz puff pastry
1 egg
oil for frying

The Stuffing
110g/4 oz white breadcrumbs
25g/1 oz butter
1 shallot, chopped
1 tablespoon chopped mint
1 tablespoon chopped parsley
1 clove garlic, crushed
salt and pepper

The Sauce
275ml/½ pint orange juice
2 tablespoons brandy
rind and segments of 1 orange
1 tablespoon tomato purée
1 tablespoon Demerara sugar
salt and pepper

Method
- Divide the lamb into two portions.
- Cut a pocket in each lamb fillet.
- To make the stuffing: gently fry the shallot in a little butter, stir in the breadcrumbs, herbs and seasoning and mix well, binding the stuffing with a little egg.
- Place the stuffing in the lamb pockets and tie with string.
- Heat a little oil in a frying pan and fry the fillet on both sides until brown. This helps to prevent the flavour of the lamb from seeping into the pastry. Leave to cool then remove the string.
- Roll out the pastry to an oblong shape and cut into long strips about 2.5cm/1" wide. Wrap around the fillets, overlapping each strip as if you were making cream horns.
- Place on a baking tray and brush with beaten egg. Bake at 200C/400F/Gas 6 for about 20 minutes.
- To make the sauce: place all the ingredients into a saucepan, omitting the brandy and orange segments and rind. Bring to the boil and simmer for 5 minutes until it has reduced slightly, and thickened.
- Pour in the brandy and orange segments and rind, and season to taste.
- Serve the lamb on a dinner plate with a little sauce around it.
- Note: you could just roll a square of pastry and wrap the lamb like a parcel.

Braised Pigeon (p. 57).

Individual Turkey Rolls (p. 61).

Peppered Beef and Vegetable Pie with Potato and Celeriac Topping (p. 64).

Pan Fried Welsh Pork with Juicy Plums (p. 68).

Venison Pâté and Cumberland Sauce (p. 77).

Stuffed Welsh Lamb Fillet in Puff Pastry (p. 80).

Lemon Meringue Tartlets with Chocolate Sauce (p. 90).

Sticky Toffee Pudding (p. 96).

BEEF CASSEROLE AND DUMPLINGS

Casseroles are comforting food. 'Cawl' and 'lobscows' have always been popular in Wales, especially in hard times. This is a very luxurious casserole, perfect for a dinner party, and best prepared early, which gives you time to get ready and relax.

Ingredients
900g/2 lbs sirloin steak, cut into large cubes
450g/1 lb button onions
450g/1 lb baby carrots
225g/8 oz button mushrooms
4 sticks celery, finely diced
3 cloves garlic, crushed
juice and rind of 2 oranges
425ml/¾ pint red wine
sprig of thyme and sage
2 tablespoons olive oil
25g/1 oz butter
50g/2 oz plain flour
salt and pepper to season

The Dumplings
175g/6 oz shredded suet
175g/6 oz self-raising flour
1 teaspoon dried thyme
1 teaspoon dried sage
a little water to mix
salt and pepper

Method
- Toss the steak in the flour. Melt the oil and butter in a large frying pan. Fry the meat in the sizzling fat to seal. Place in a large casserole dish.

- Cook the cleaned vegetables whole in the remaining fat. Add the garlic, herbs, orange juice and rind and cook for about 5 minutes.

- Add the vegetables to the casserole and mix well.

- Season to taste, pour in the wine and cook at 180C/350F/Gas 4 for about 1 hour.

- To make the dumplings: mix all the dry ingredients together.

- Add a little water to bind the dry mixture. Divide into 12 small dumplings, drop into the piping hot casserole and cook for a further 20 minutes.

- To serve: sprinkle with plenty of chopped parsley.

QUICK AND EASY SPONGE

Special occasions are sometimes last-minute events. Some people are wary of making a sponge, they tell me, because they think it will curdle. This is a very quick, successful way of avoiding pitfalls!

Ingredients
225g/8 oz soft Welsh butter
225g/8 oz caster sugar
4 medium eggs
225g/8 oz self-raising flour
1 teaspoon baking powder
1 teaspoon vanilla essence

The Filling
110g/4 oz Welsh cream cheese
150ml/¼ pint double cream, whipped
segments of 1 orange
2 passion fruit

Method
- Grease and line the bottom of two 20cm/8" sponge tins.
- Place the flour, baking powder, butter, sugar, eggs and vanilla essence in a large mixing bowl.
- With an electric whisk, beat all the ingredients together on a slow speed until it is evenly mixed, and of a dropping consistency. Divide the mixture between the two tins and spread evenly.
- Cook at 180C/350F/Gas 4 for 20-25 minutes.
- Cool on a wire tray then remove the paper.
- To make the filling: mix together the cream cheese, whipped cream and orange rind.
- Spread the filling on one sponge. Top with the orange segments and the pulp of the passion fruit.
- Place the remaining sponge on top and dust with icing sugar.

HOT CROSS BUNS

Good Friday always reminds me of my mother. She would already have prepared the Hot Cross Buns on the Thursday, ready for the day itself. The smell of yeast and baking wafting through the air was heavenly. Why not try out this recipe of mine and give a neighbour or an elderly relative or friend a little treat?

Ingredients
450g/1 lb strong plain flour
50g/2 oz melted butter
50g/2 oz caster sugar
150ml/¼ pint warm milk
1 teaspoon mixed spice
50g/2 oz currants or sultanas
1 tablespoon marmalade
pinch of salt
2 eggs
25g/1 oz fresh yeast or 2 sachets
   easy-blend dried yeast

The Glaze
2 tablespoons caster sugar
4 tablespoons water

Method
- Place the flour in a large bowl. Add the sugar, spice, salt, sultanas and dried yeast and mix well. If using fresh yeast, add 1 teaspoon caster sugar and 1 teaspoon cream, leave until it becomes liquid and pour in with the milk.

- Make a well in the mixture, pour in the melted butter, warm milk, marmalade and two beaten eggs. Using a little extra flour, knead the dough for 2-3 minutes until smooth.

- Leave the dough overnight to rise.

- The following day, divide the dough into 12 buns and lightly knead each one, making a cross on the top of each one with a knife.

- Place the dough on a greased tray, cover with a cloth or place the tray in a plastic bag and leave to rise in a warm place until the buns double in size. An hour should be enough.

- Cook at 200C/400F/Gas 6 for 15-20 minutes.

- To make the glaze: place the sugar and water in a saucepan and boil for 2-3 minutes. Brush onto the buns while hot.

MINCEMEAT

The phrase 'mincemeat' is very misleading, when all the ingredients are fruits of the earth! It is easy to whip up a batch if you need to make quick presents or you want to make the cake on the next page! Why not make some and keep it in the pantry in case of emergencies?

Ingredients
450g/1 lb sultanas
450g/1 lb small raisins
450g/1 lb currants
225g/8 oz glacé cherries, chopped
225g/8 oz ready-to-eat apricots, chopped
rind and juice of 1 orange
rind and juice of 1 lemon
350g/12 oz butter
350g/12 oz dark soft brown sugar
1 teaspoon cinammon
1 teaspoon mixed spice
425ml/¾ pint Cwm Deri hazelnut liqueur or 425ml/¾ pint brandy

Method
- Place the butter and sugar in a heavy-based saucepan and gently melt over a low heat.

- Using a large mixing bowl, mix together the dried fruits, orange and lemon juices and rinds, and the spices.

- Pour the melted sugar and butter into the mixture and mix thoroughly.

- Finally, pour in the liqueur and stir well. At this point you may think it is too runny, *but* leave it covered in the bowl overnight and, by the morning, the fruit will have absorbed all the liquid – as if by magic!

- Spoon into clean, sterilised jars, seal and label. Store in a cool, dry place and use in mince pies or a quick Christmas cake.

MINCEMEAT CAKE

Ingredients
900g/2 lbs mincemeat
225g/8 oz butter, softened
225g/8 oz soft brown sugar
4 eggs
175g/6 oz plain flour
175g/6 oz self-raising flour
50g/2 oz ground almonds
1 tablespoon black treacle
1 teaspoon mixed spice

Method
- Beat together the butter and sugar until you have a dropping consistency.

- Beat in the eggs whole, one at a time.

- Stir in the flour, ground almonds and spice.

- Melt the treacle, and stir into the mixture.

- Mix in the mincemeat, mixing well to ensure it is all evenly mixed through.

- Divide the mixture between two lined 18cm/7" cake tins, or one 23cm/9" tin. Spread the top evenly.

- Cook at 150C/300F/Gas 2 for 1½ hours (if using a large tin, cook for 2½-3 hours).

- Place flaked almonds on top to make a Dundee cake, or leave plain for icing.

SWEETS

Pudding, dessert, whatever you call it, there's many a sweet-toothed person out there who thinks a meal is not complete unless followed by something sweet! I have deliberately chosen a wide variety of sweets, some cakes, some traditional Welsh recipes with my own twist, and several heavenly treats!

SULTANA AND WALNUT *BARA BRITH*

Bara brith *is a traditional type of tea bread made here in Wales. It is usually served with lashings of Welsh butter. It certainly makes a substantial and delicious addition for any tea table. Some recipes use yeast while others simply soak the fruit in cold tea, usually adding nuts.*

Ingredients
175g/6 oz butter
175g/6 oz Demerara sugar
2 eggs
450g/1 lb self-raising flour
1 teaspoon mixed spice
50g/2 oz chopped walnuts
175g/6 oz sultanas
150ml/¼ pint apple juice
1 tablespoon black treacle
pinch of salt

Method
- Into a large saucepan, pour the apple juice, add the butter, sugar and treacle. Heat until the butter and sugar have melted, then simmer for 2-3 minutes.

- Leave to cool, then beat in the eggs, mix in the flour, sultanas, spice and walnuts.

- Grease and line two 450g/1 lb loaf tins, and divide the mixture between them. Using a spatula, smooth the top, then sprinkle a little Demerara sugar on top; this gives a lovely crunchy topping.

- Bake for about 1½ hours at 150C/300F/Gas 2. It should be firm to the touch. Leave to cool before removing from the tin.

- To serve: cut into slices with butter; this is a matter of choice.

- Note: orange juice or cold tea can be used to replace the apple juice.

CARAMELISED APPLE AND RAISIN TART

Apples are extremely versatile and nutritious. Their texture varies from silken to mealy, giving an eating experience from thrilling to plain dull. There are so many varieties available today, that we are spoilt for choice. The apple is indeed a sign of fertility and good luck! This is one of my favourite recipes.

Ingredients
350g/12oz strong plain flour
175g/6 oz butter
175g/6 oz caster sugar
3 egg yolks

The Filling
4-6 Golden Delicious apples
50g/2 oz Demerara sugar
50g/2 oz butter
6 cloves
110g/4 oz small raisins
1 lemon

Method
- Cream the butter and sugar, then beat in the egg yolks.

- Add the flour and mix well into the creamed butter and sugar. Knead lightly to bind to a dough, then leave for 15 minutes to relax.

- To make the filling: melt the butter in a large saucepan or frying pan, then add the sugar.

- Now add the prepared apples, peeled, cored and cut into quarters. Gently toss the apples in the sugar and melted butter and cook for about 5 minutes, then mix in the raisins, cloves, lemon juice and rind.

- To make an old-fashioned-looking tart, use an ovenproof plate about 25.5cm/10" in diameter. Use half the pastry to line the plate. Spoon on the apple mixture, then roll the remaining pastry and cover the top. Press the edges gently, and use the palm of your hands to trim any excess pastry. Brush the top with water and sprinkle on some caster sugar; this gives a lovely crunchy texture.

- Bake for 20-30 minutes at 180C/350F/Gas 4.

- Serve with organic yogurt or cream.

- Note: use the palm of your hands to trim the pastry when making tarts, because the pastry does not shrink as it does when using a knife.

LEMON MERINGUE TARTLETS WITH CHOCOLATE SAUCE

Ingredients

Basic Sweet Pastry
275g/10 oz plain flour
175g/6 oz butter
50g/2 oz caster sugar
2 egg yolks
4 tablespoons cold water (approx.)

Chocolate Sauce
275ml/½ pint double cream
225g/8 oz good-quality chocolate

The Filling
150ml/¼ pint water
50g/2 oz butter
juice and rind of 2 lemons
1 level tablespoon cornflour
50g/2 oz caster sugar
2 egg yolks

The Meringue
2 egg whites
110g/4 oz caster sugar

Method
- To make the pastry: cream the butter and sugar, then beat in the egg yolks. Stir in the flour, add a little water, then mix well until the pastry becomes quite smooth and not sticky. Leave to chill for 15 minutes before rolling.

- Roll the pastry to about 5mm/¼" thickness then cut to the size of your tartlet tins. Line the inside with greaseproof paper or crinkled foil and cook for 10 minutes at 180C/350F/Gas 4. Remove the foil and cook for a further 3-4 minutes. When cool, gently remove from the tin.

- To make the filling: place the water, butter, sugar, juice and rind of lemons in a pan, bring to the boil, then thicken by blending the cornflour with a little water and pour into the saucepan. Beat in the egg yolks and cook for 2-3 minutes. Divide the filling between 6 tartlets.

- To make the meringue: whisk the two egg whites until firm, then gradually whisk in the caster sugar and beat the meringue until glossy.

- Top each tartlet with meringue, cook in the oven for 5 minutes at 180C/ 350F/Gas 4 until golden brown, or place under the grill to brown.

- To make the sauce: gently bring the chocolate and cream to the boil and whisk or stir while the chocolate melts.

- Serve one tartlet per person, pour the sauce around and decorate with a sliced, fanned strawberry. Dust with icing sugar or cocoa.

RASPBERRY AND ALMOND PUDDING

This is an excellent pudding for coeliacs, who have an intolerance to gluten, so that they cannot eat wheat, rye, barley, oats, or anything containing them. Here we use ground almonds which give a delicious flavour.

Ingredients
110g/4 oz ground almonds
50g/2 oz butter
50g/2 oz caster sugar
4 tablespoons raspberry jam (preferably home-made)
a few drops almond essence
2 eggs

Method
- Grease four ramekin dishes with butter.

- Place a tablespoon of jam in each.

- Cream the butter and sugar until light and fluffy, then beat in the egg yolks and almond essence. Now mix in the ground almonds.

- Whisk the egg whites until firm, then fold into the mixture. Divide the mixture into the ramekins, and cover each with buttered foil. Place the dishes into a saucepan, pour in boiling water to half way up the dishes. Cover and simmer for 30-35 minutes.

- To serve: remove the foil and turn the puddings upside down onto a serving plate.

- Serve with natural yogurt or crème fraîche.

- Note: any jam can be used, especially home-made plum jam, strawberry jam, blackcurrant jam, etc.

CHOCOLATE APRICOT PUDDING

This is a delicious winter pudding. It's a good alternative for Christmas Day, served with chocolate sauce or crème fraîche. The most important thing is to make it with good-quality chocolate containing minimum 70% cocoa solids.

Ingredients

The Pudding
110g/4 oz soft Welsh butter
110g/4 oz soft dark brown sugar
2 medium eggs
1 tablespoon apricot jam
110g/4 oz self-raising flour
50g/2 oz ground almonds
110g/4 oz dark or milk chocolate
2 tablespoons brandy

The Sauce
200g/7 oz dark chocolate
275ml/½ pint double cream

Method
- Cut the chocolate into pieces, place in a basin with the brandy, then place the basin over a saucepan of hot water to melt the chocolate. Do not over-heat, or it will spoil.

- Cream together the butter and sugar, and gradually beat in the eggs. Mix in the apricot jam and the melted chocolate and brandy. Fold in the flour and ground almonds.

- Divide the mixture into four small greased pudding basins (such as ramekin dishes), or a 20cm x 15cm/8" x 6" gratin dish.

- Cook for about 30 minutes at 180C/350F/Gas 4.

- To make the sauce: place the ingredients in a saucepan and gently heat until the chocolate has melted.

- Serve the pudding hot with the warm chocolate sauce.

ORGANIC YOGURT CAKE

This is especially for people who are not experts in making cakes. I suggest you try this simple, deliciously tasty cake and really surprise your friends!

Ingredients
350g/12oz self-raising flour
225g/8 oz caster sugar
150ml/¼ pint natural organic yogurt
150ml/¼ pint light olive oil
1 teaspoon vanilla essence
3 large eggs
110g/4 oz ground almonds

Method
- Place the flour, sugar and ground almonds in a bowl.

- Spoon in the yogurt and pour in the oil.

- Beat the eggs lightly, then add the vanilla essence.

- Using a wooden spoon, mix all the ingredients well, and beat for 2-3 minutes.

- Pour into a round, lined 20cm/8" cake tin or a 900g/2 lb loaf tin.

- Cook for 1 hour at 170C/325F/Gas 3.

- If you wish, you can sprinkle some flaked almonds and glacé cherries on the top or, for a different flavour, use the grated rind of a lemon.

GLUTEN-FREE BUTTERY LEMON SHORTBREAD

These biscuits are simply delicious, and make a terrific tea-time treat for coeliacs. They can be sandwiched together with cream and strawberries.

Ingredients
175g/6 oz butter
75g/3 oz caster sugar
rind of 1 lemon
175g/6 oz rice flour or ground rice
75g/3 oz ground almonds

Method
- Cream the butter and sugar until pale and fluffy. Mix in the lemon rind.

- Mix in the rice flour and ground almonds and knead lightly to form a smooth dough.

- Roll out the dough to 5mm/¼" thickness on a clean surface dusted with rice flour. Using a 4cm/1½" plain round cutter, make about 35 biscuits.

- Chill in the fridge for about half an hour before cooking. Bake for about 10-15 minutes at 170C/325F/Gas 3 until pale and golden, and firm to the touch.

- Leave to cool on the tray. Before serving, sprinkle with caster sugar.

QUICK AND EASY TRIFLE

Sometimes, time does not allow for elaborate preparations, so when you need to cheat, here's how!

Ingredients
1 jam Swiss roll
275ml/½ pint ready-made custard
570ml/1 pint double cream
4 tablespoons brandy
400g/14 oz tin of fruit of your choice, drained
1 chocolate flake

Method
- Cut the Swiss roll into slices and arrange in a glass bowl or individual dishes.

- Pour over some brandy and top with fruit.

- Whisk the cream until thick, then mix together the custard and cream. Spoon over the fruit. Decorate with the crushed flake.

STICKY TOFFEE PUDDING

All of us, especially children, have a favourite pudding – I know that my grandchildren do! When the weather turns cold, hot puddings are just the thing. Why not try this easy-to-cook recipe?

Ingredients

The Pudding	*The Sauce*
110g/4 oz butter	2 tablespoons golden syrup
110g/4 oz caster sugar	1 tablespoon black treacle
2 eggs	25g/1 oz butter
75g/3 oz self-raising flour	
25g/1 oz ground almonds	

Method

- To make the sauce: place all the ingredients in a saucepan and gently heat until the butter has melted, stirring constantly.

- Grease four small pudding basins, 150ml/¼ pint size, or four 7.5cm/3" ramekin dishes, then divide the sauce equally between them.

- Cream together the butter and sugar until fluffy and creamy. Beat in the eggs, then fold in the flour and ground almonds.

- Spoon the mixture into the basins, covering the syrup mixture in the bottom. Place the basins on a baking tray and cook for 20 minutes at 180C/350F/ Gas 4 until well-risen, golden and firm to the touch.

- Remove from the oven and leave to rest for 5 minutes. Then turn upside down onto a pudding plate and serve with double cream, custard or yogurt.

- Note: to make a variety of puddings from the same mixture, you could add finely-chopped nuts, 1 tablespoon lemon curd, 1 tablespoon cocoa powder, 1 tablespoon coffee or 25g/1 oz dates or sultanas.